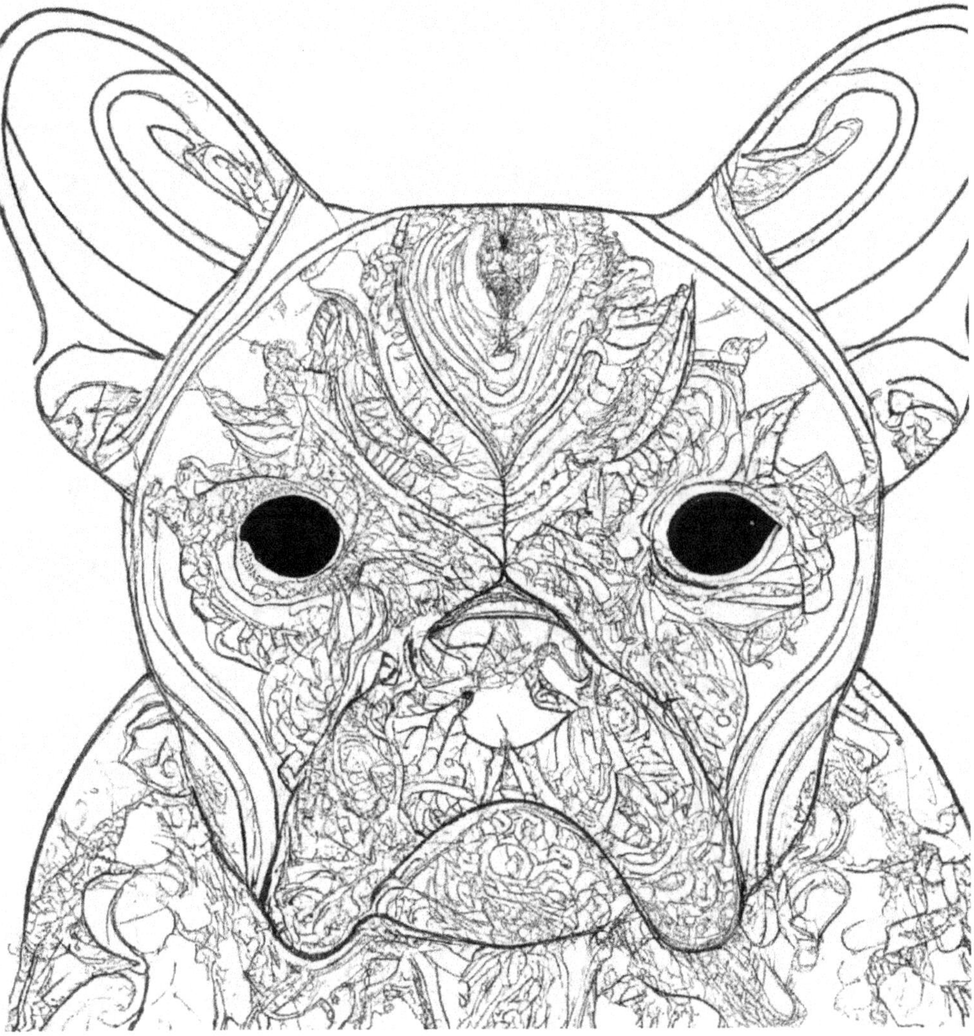

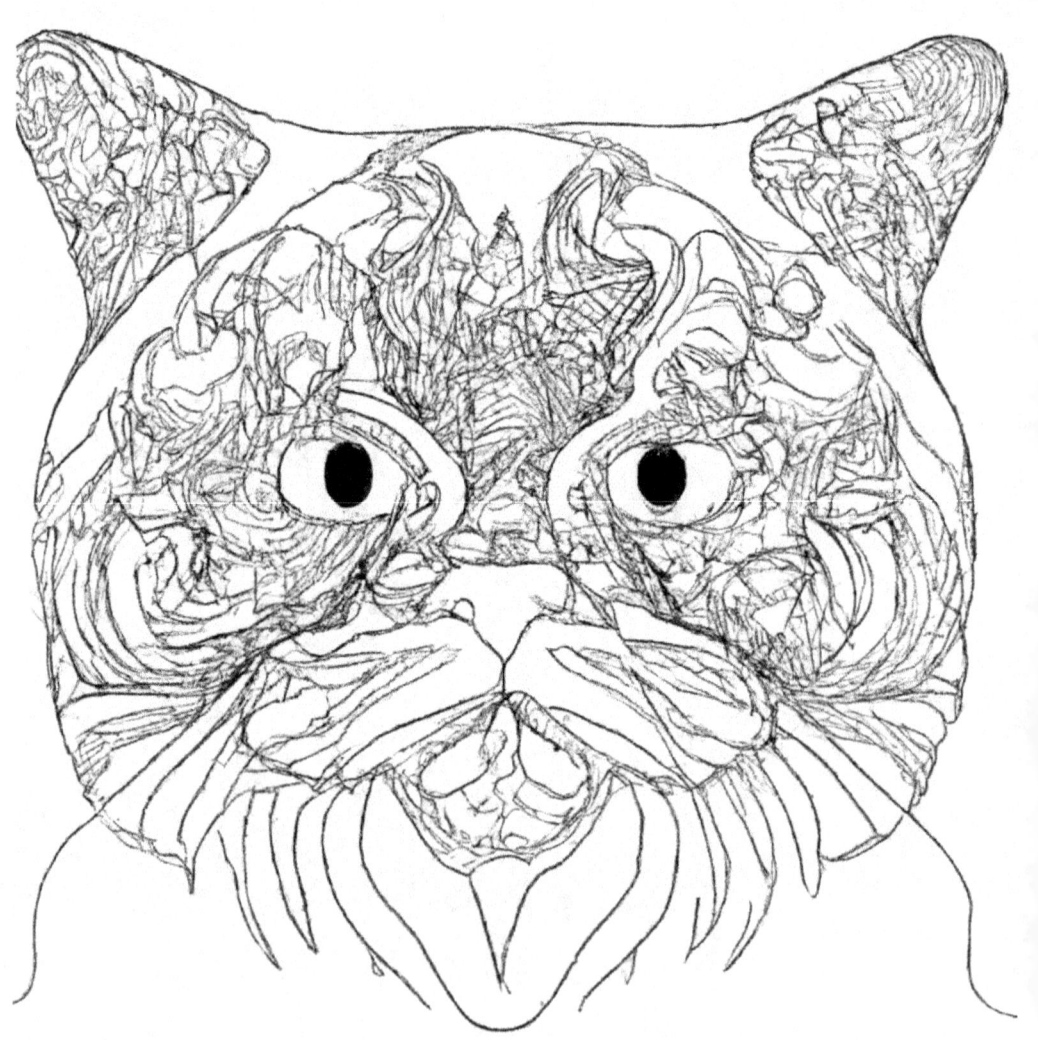

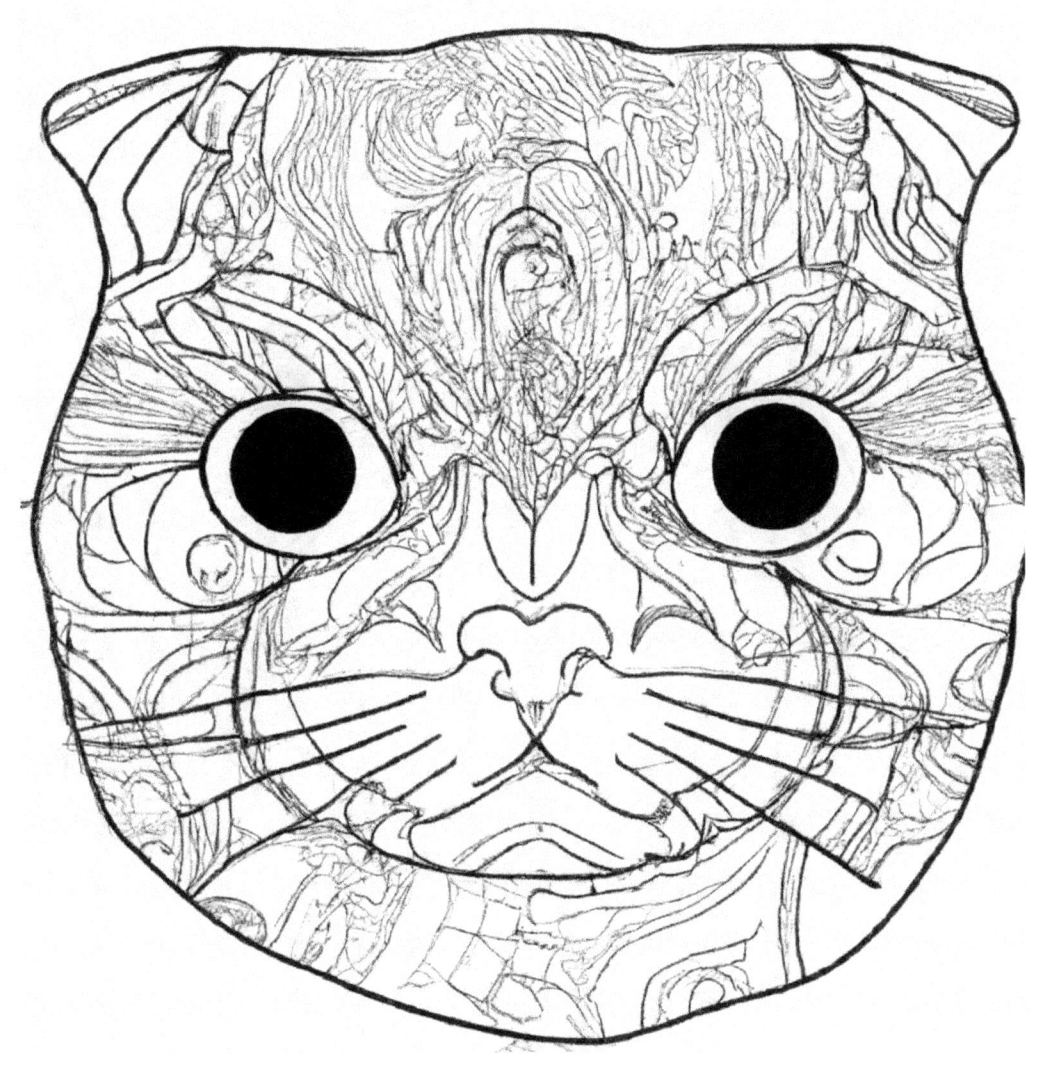

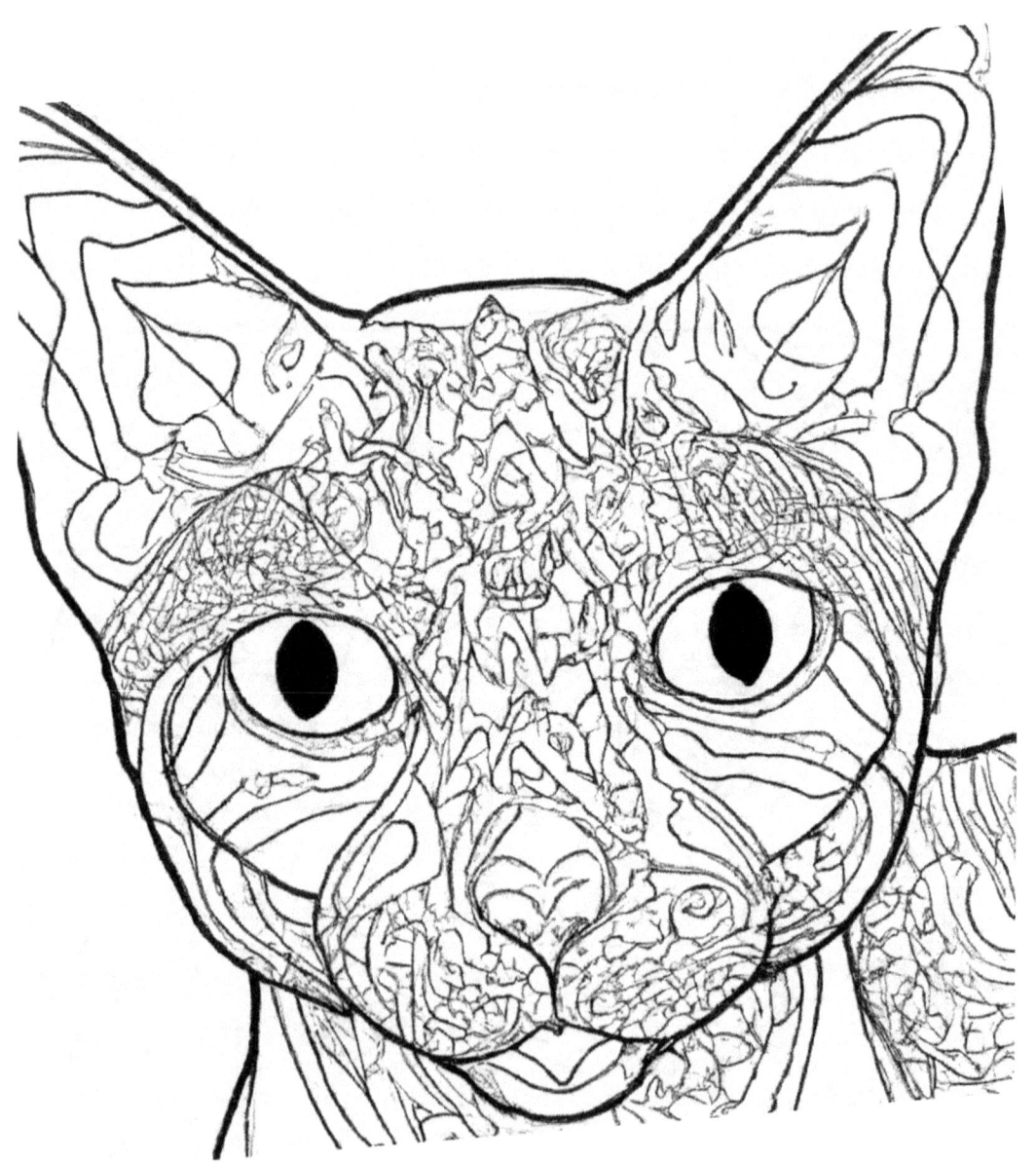

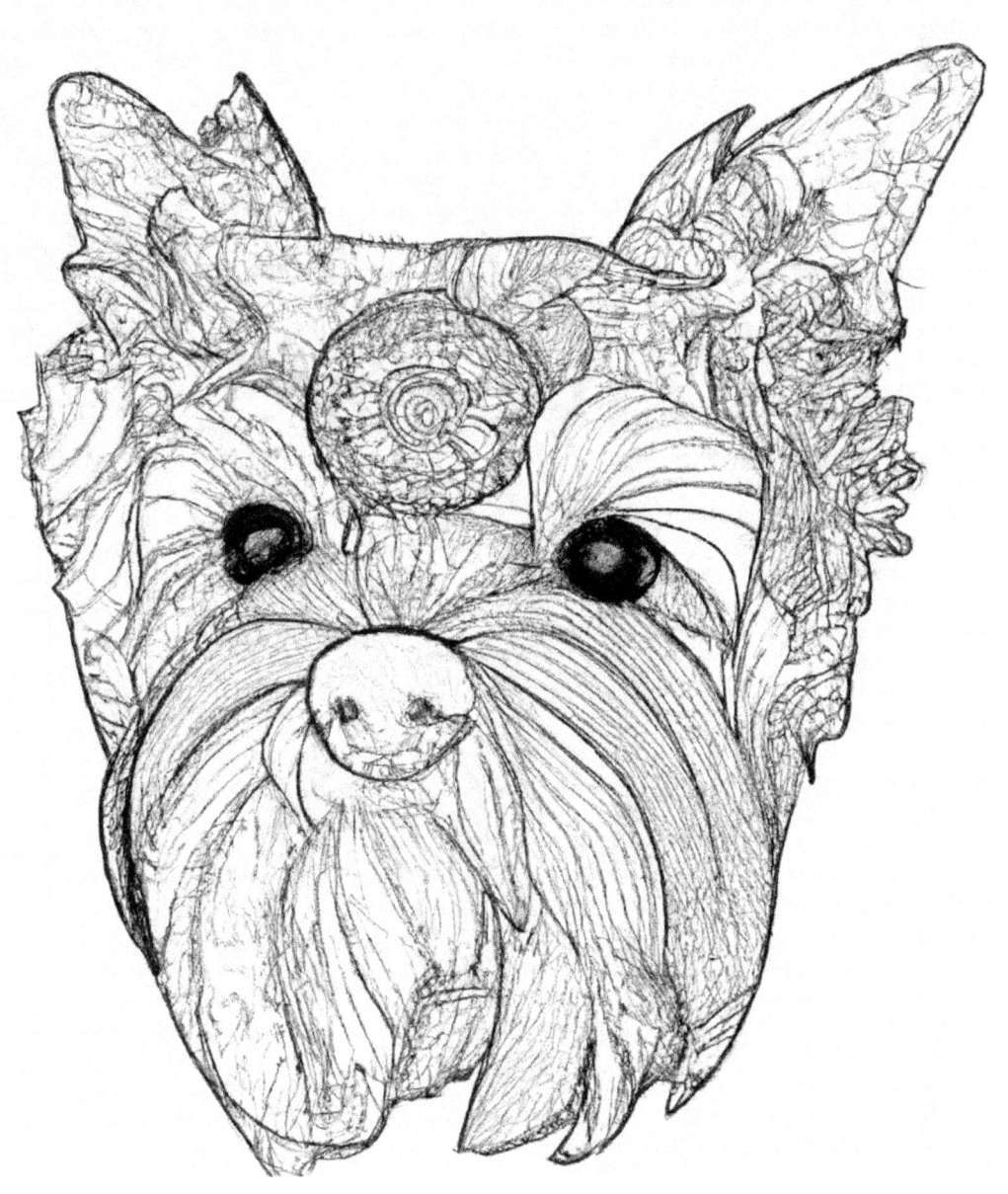

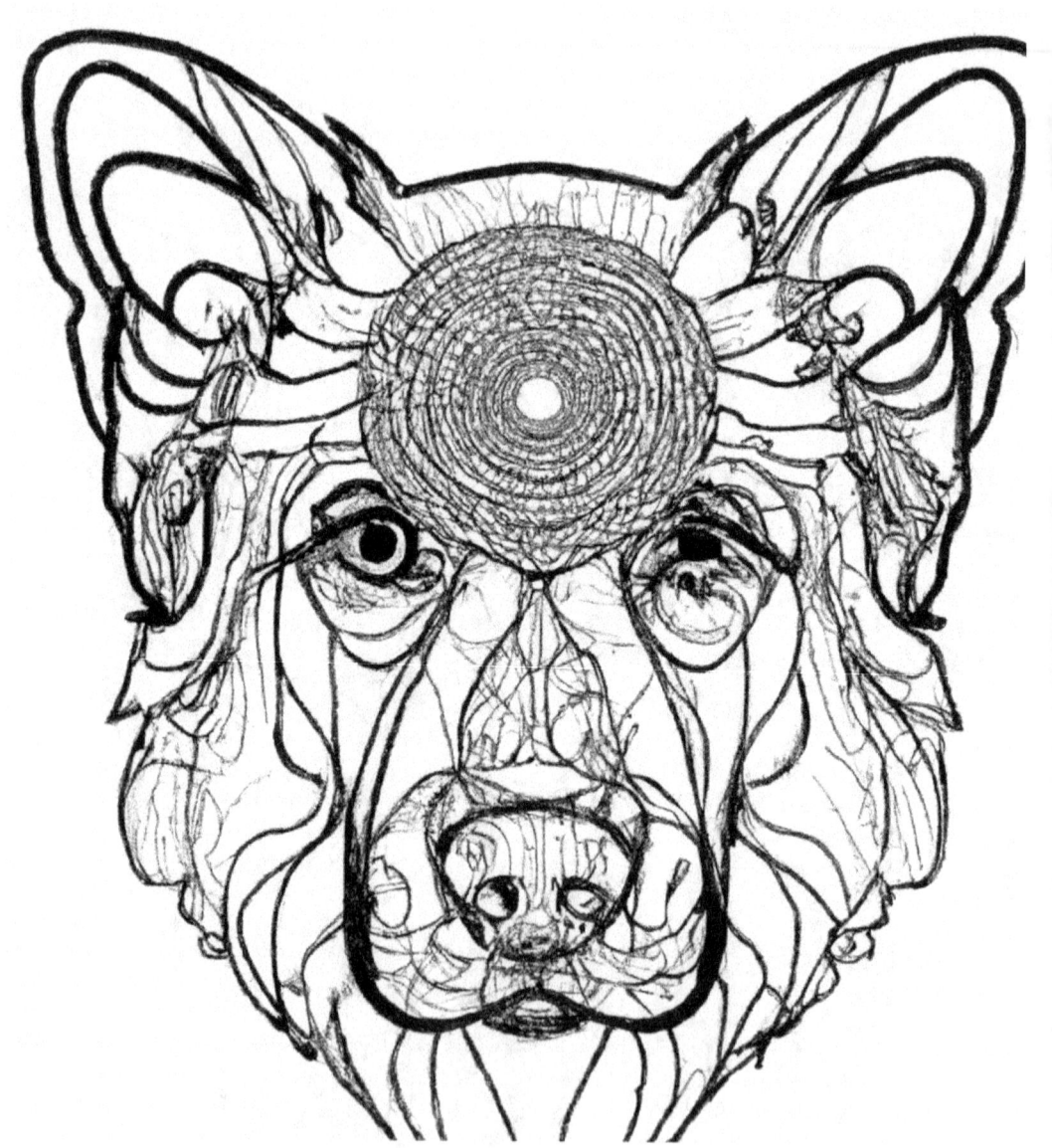

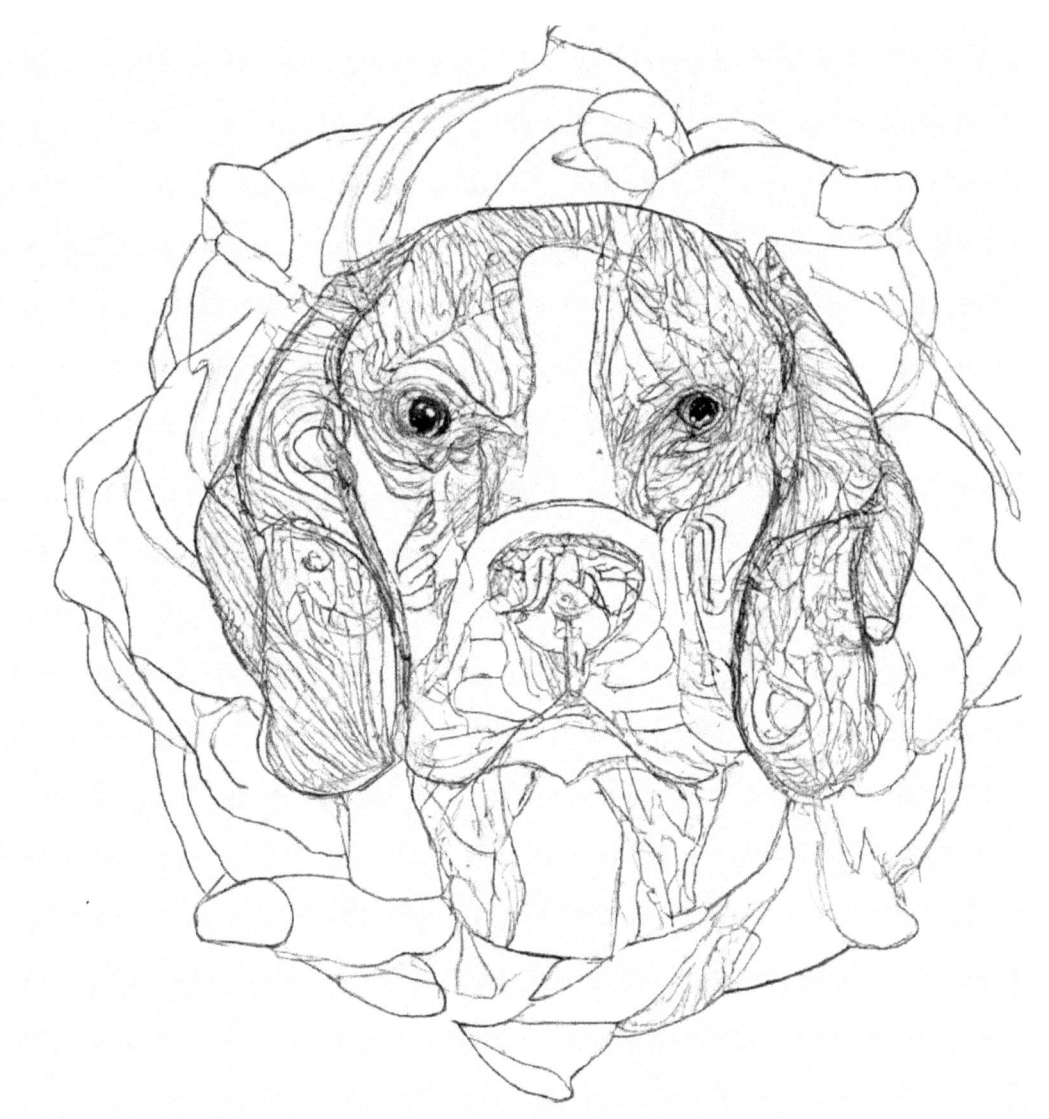

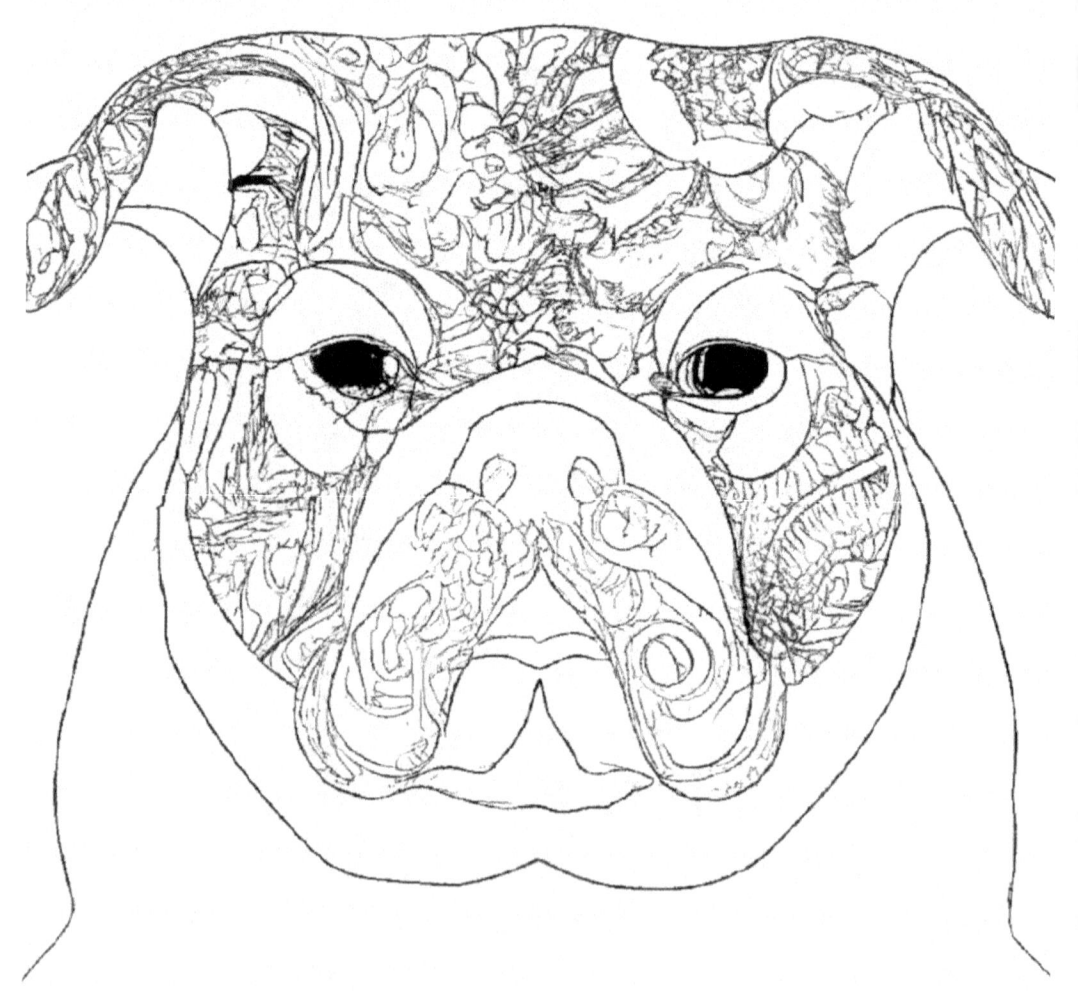

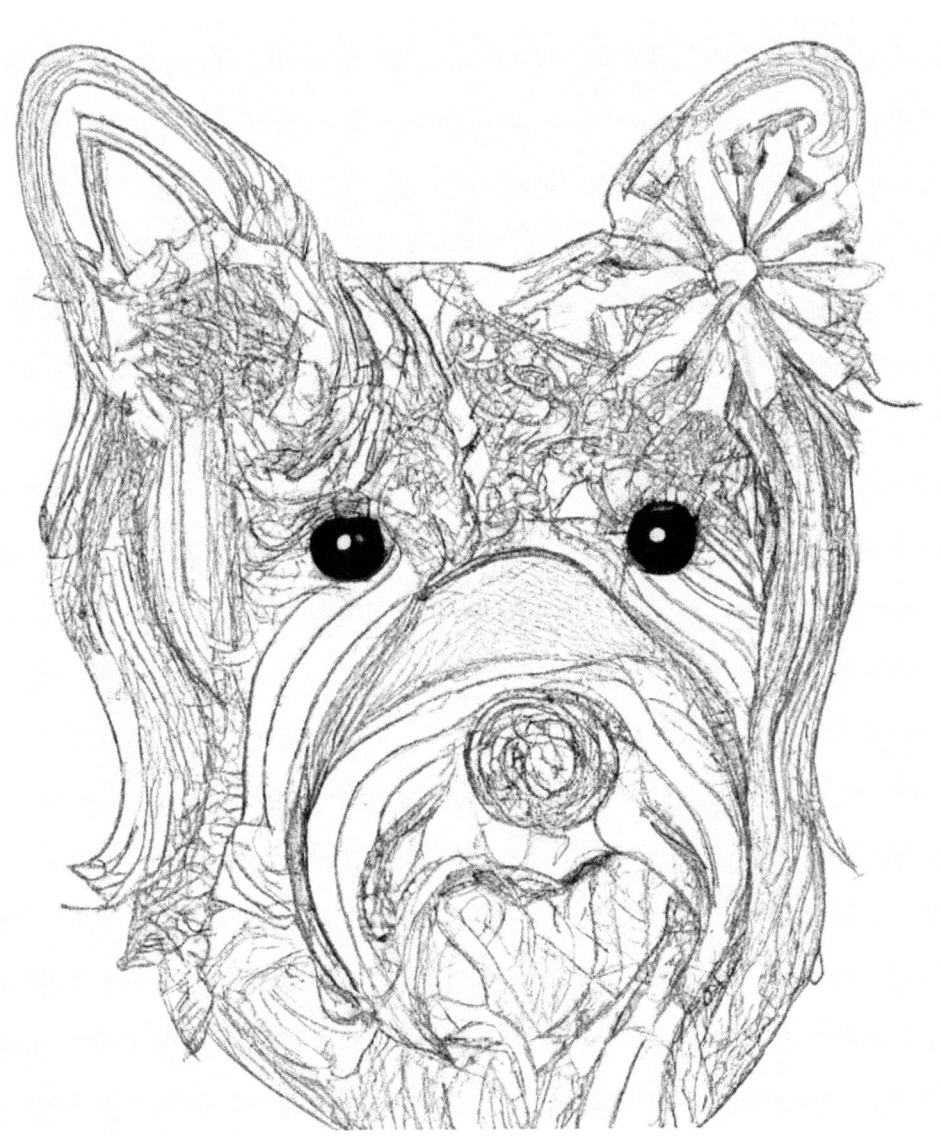

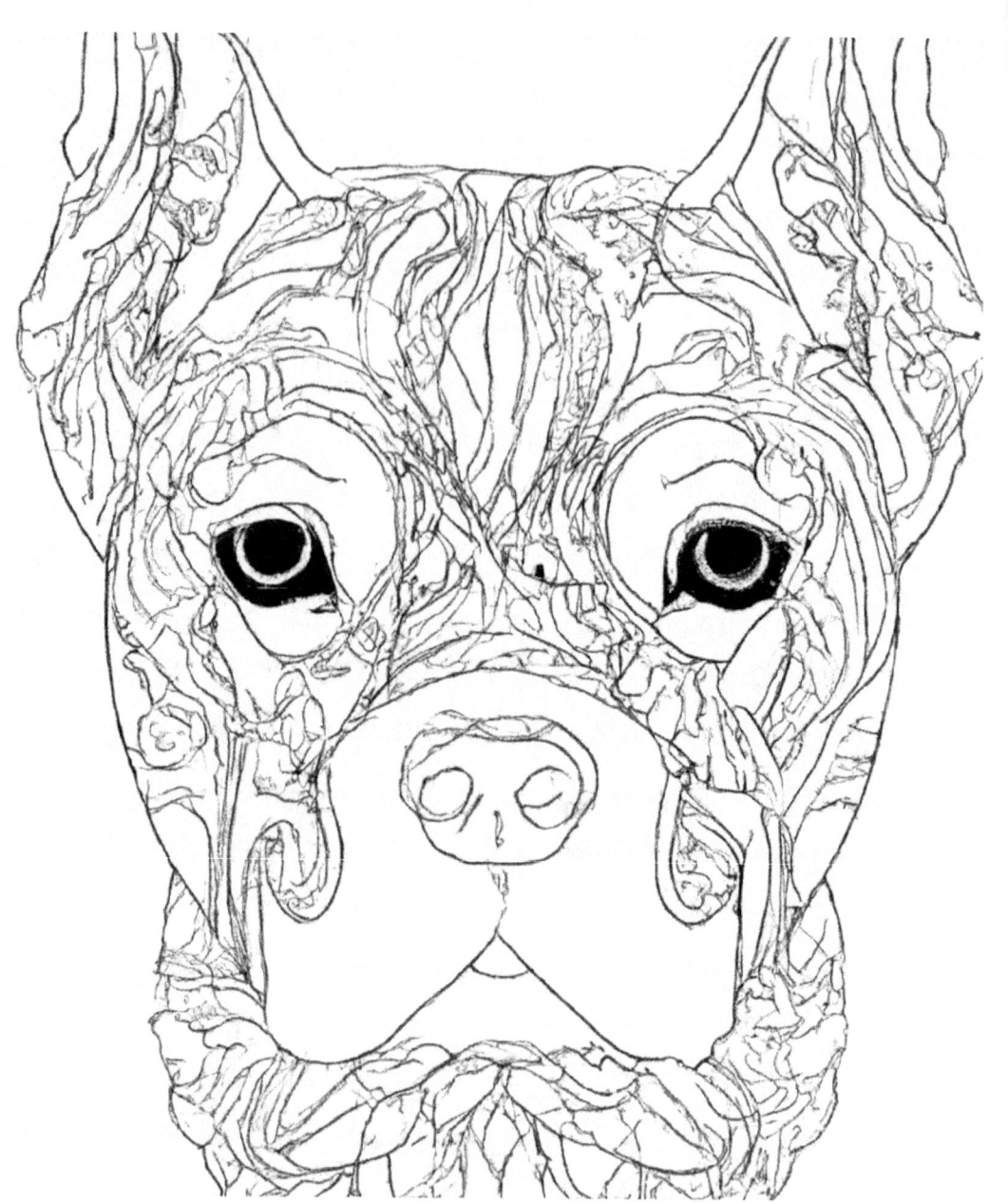

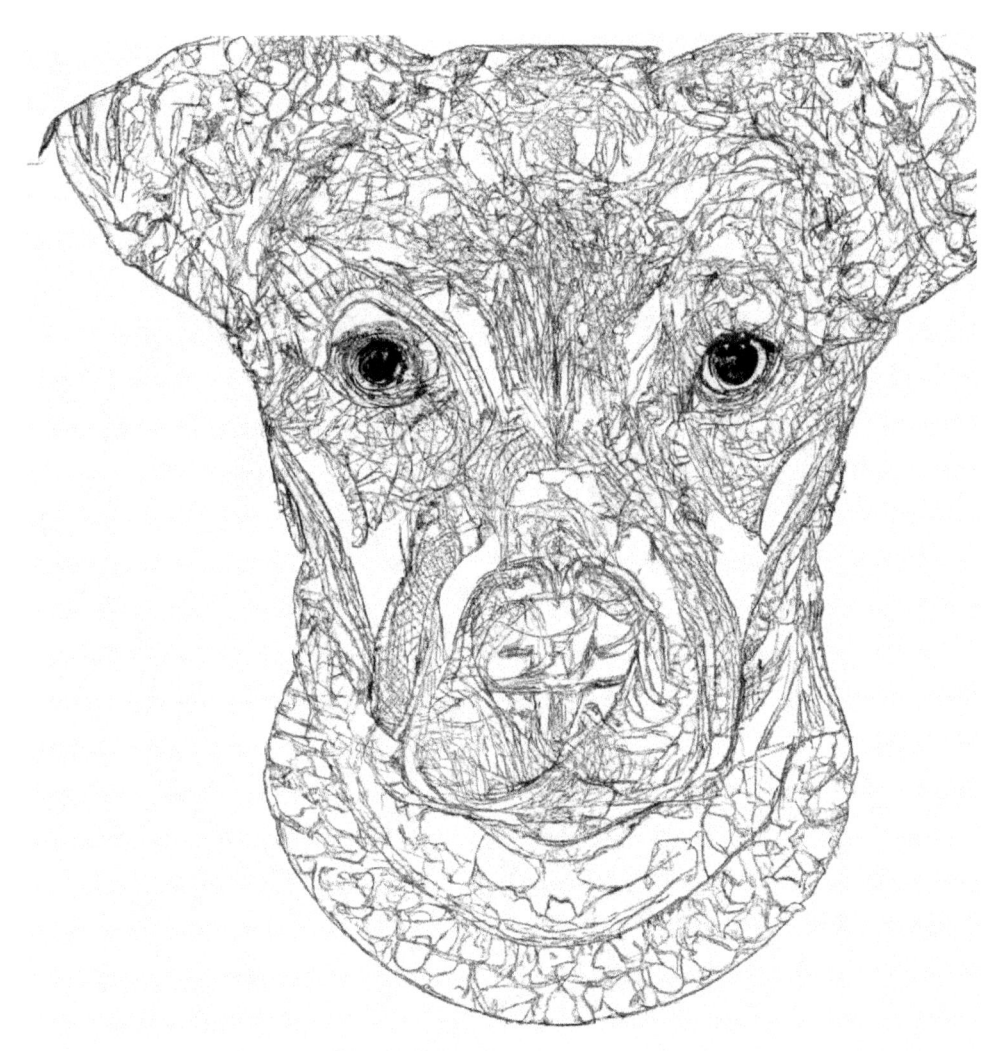

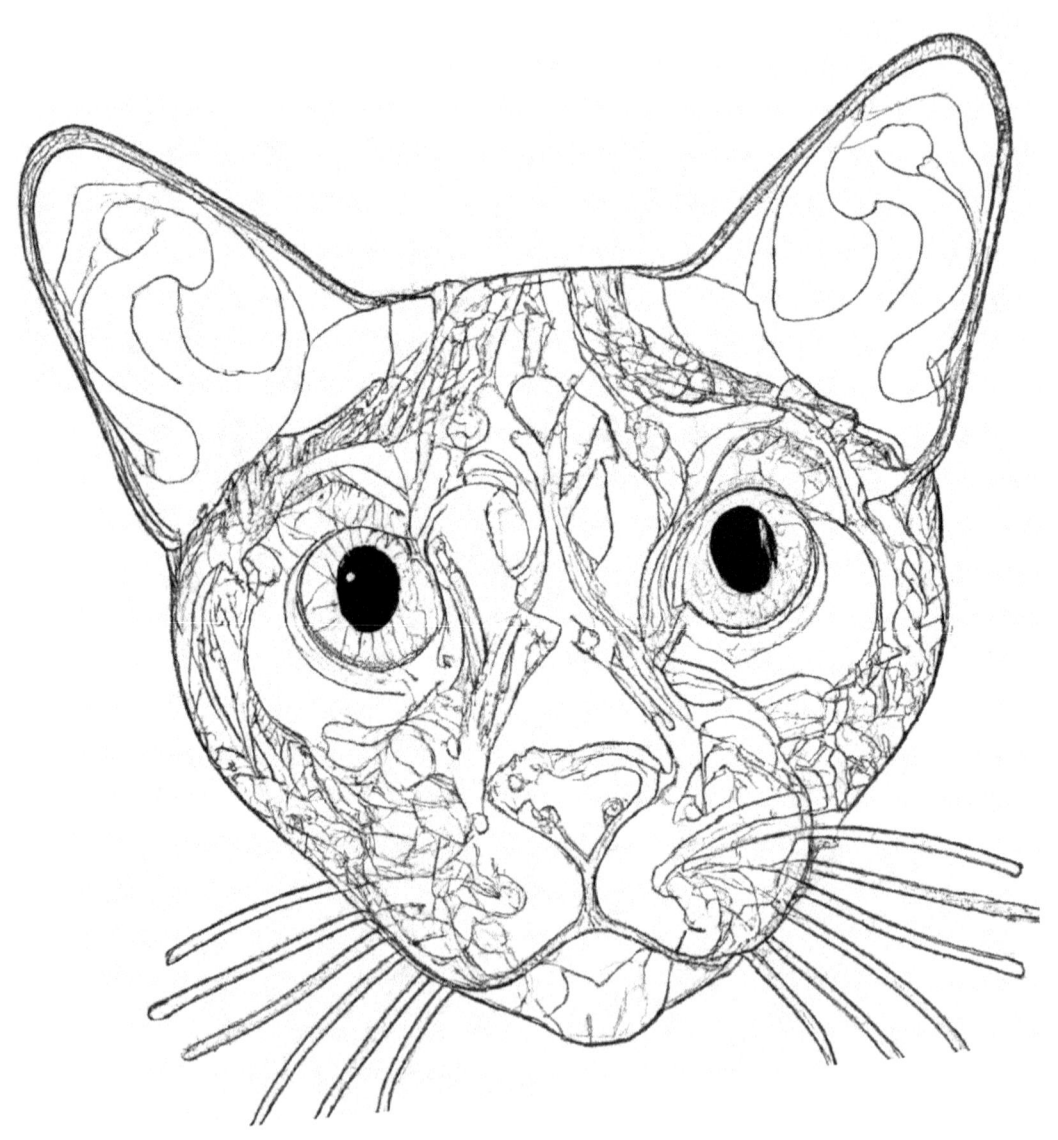

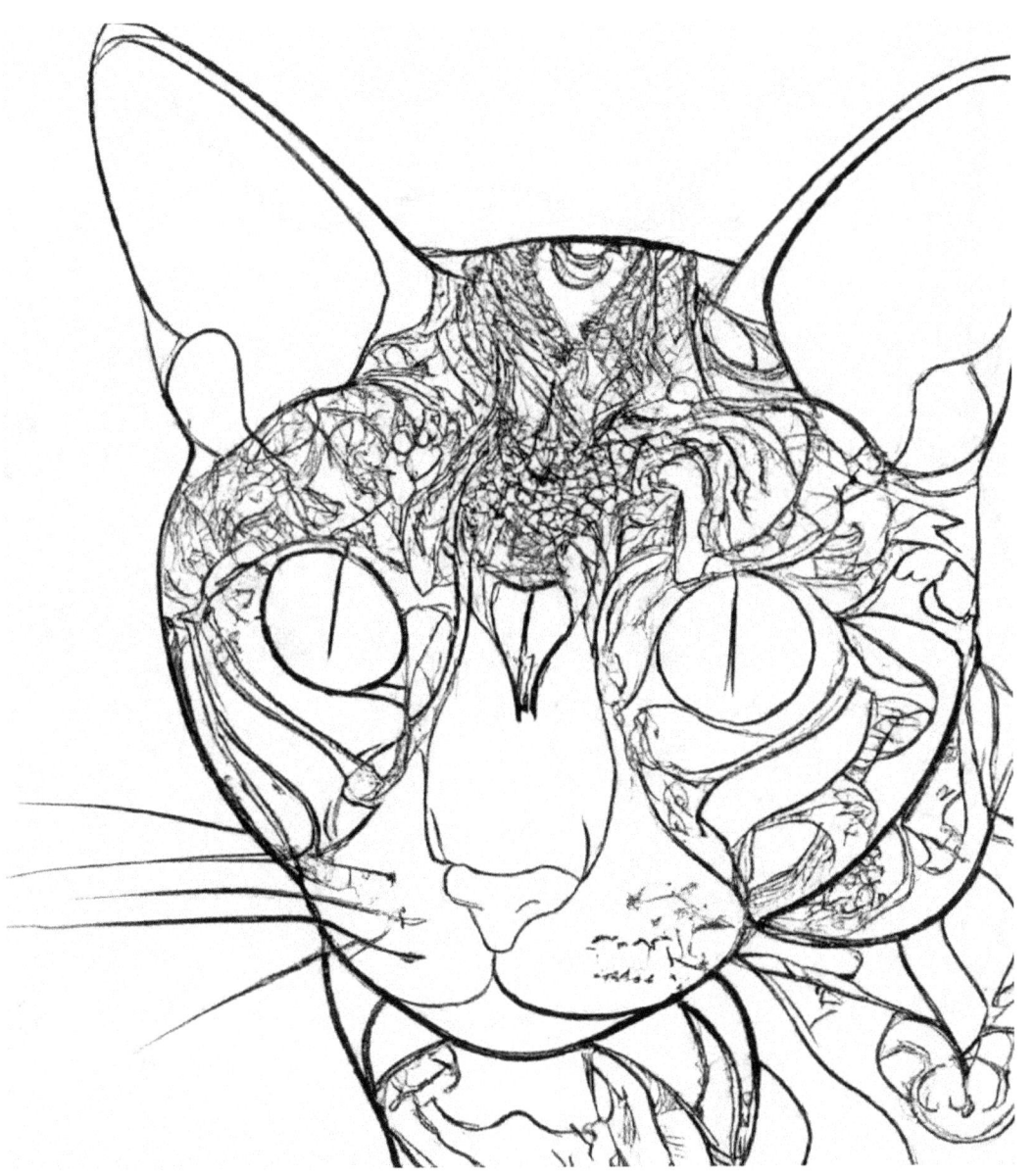

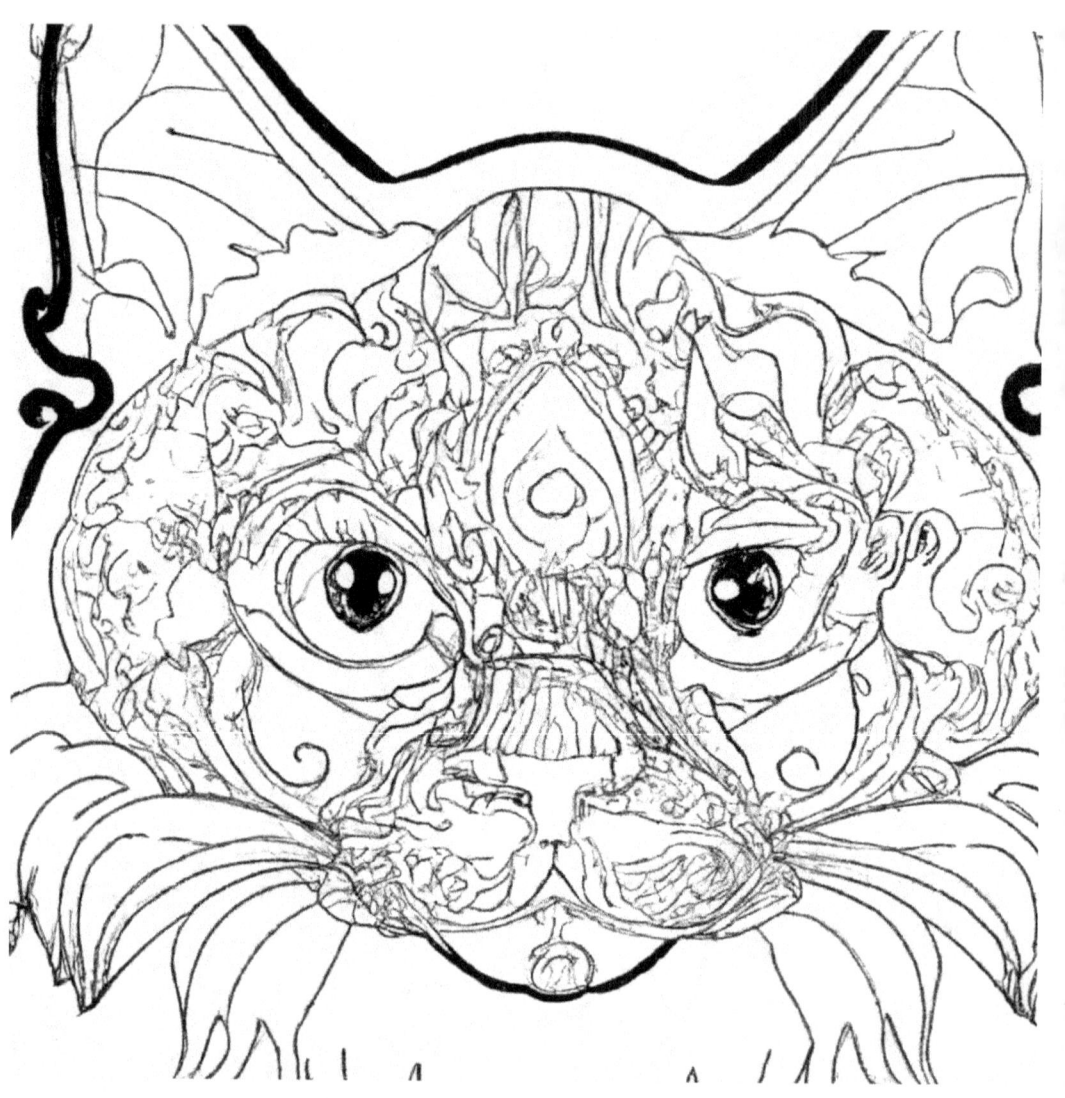

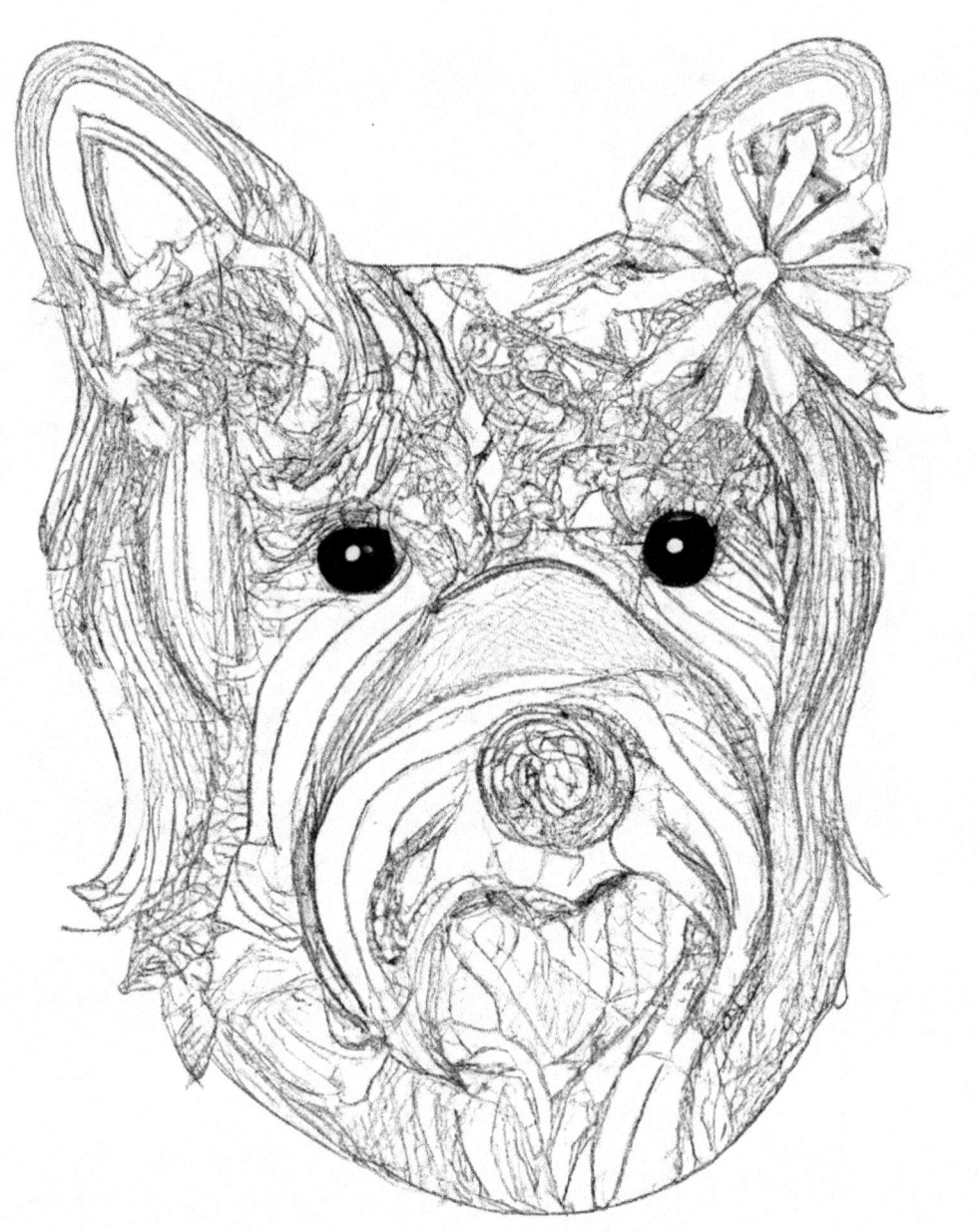

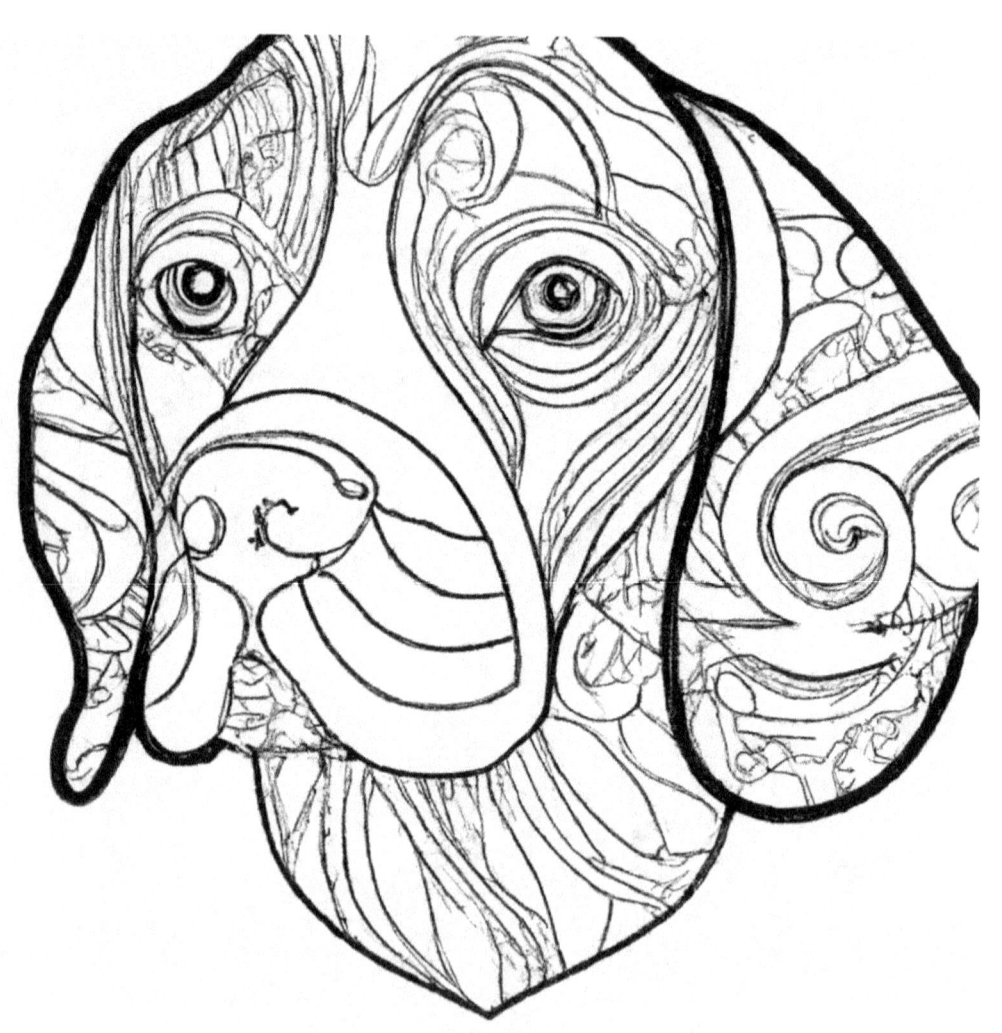

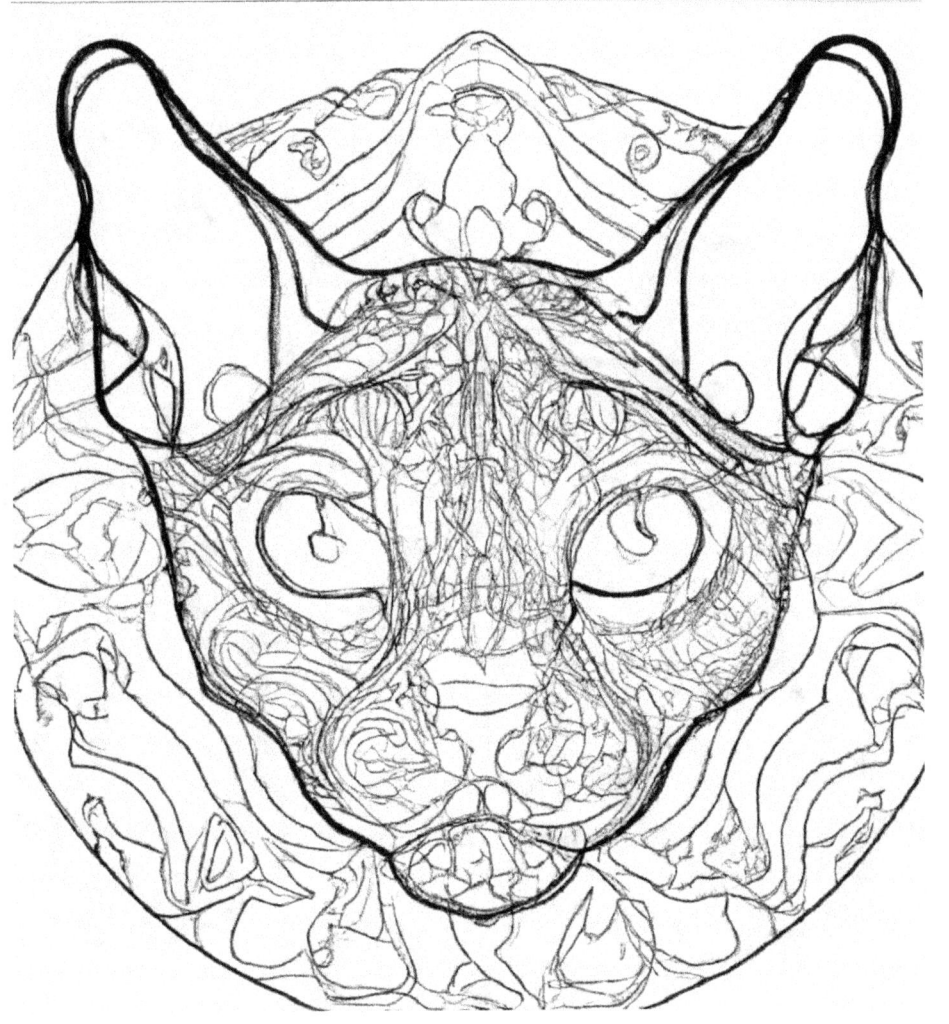

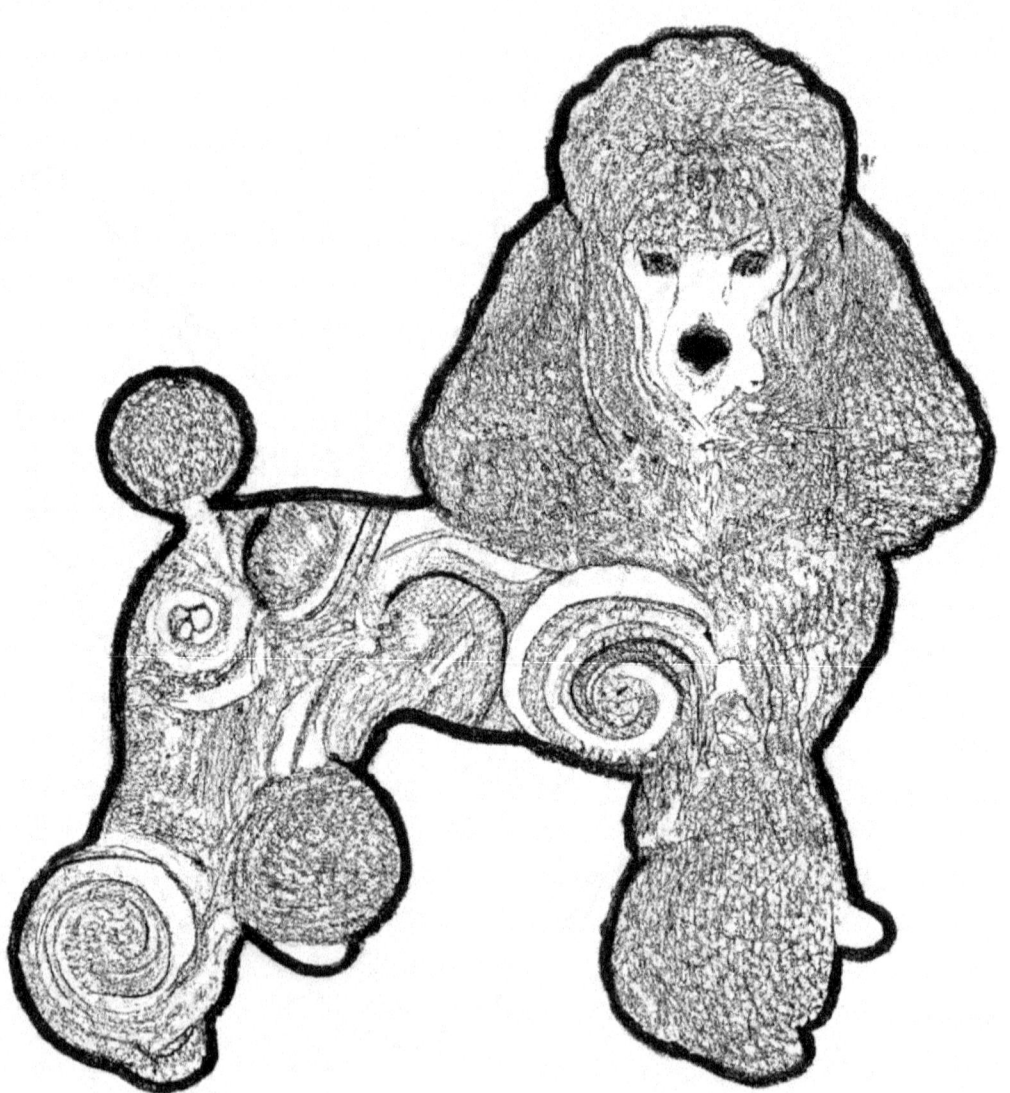

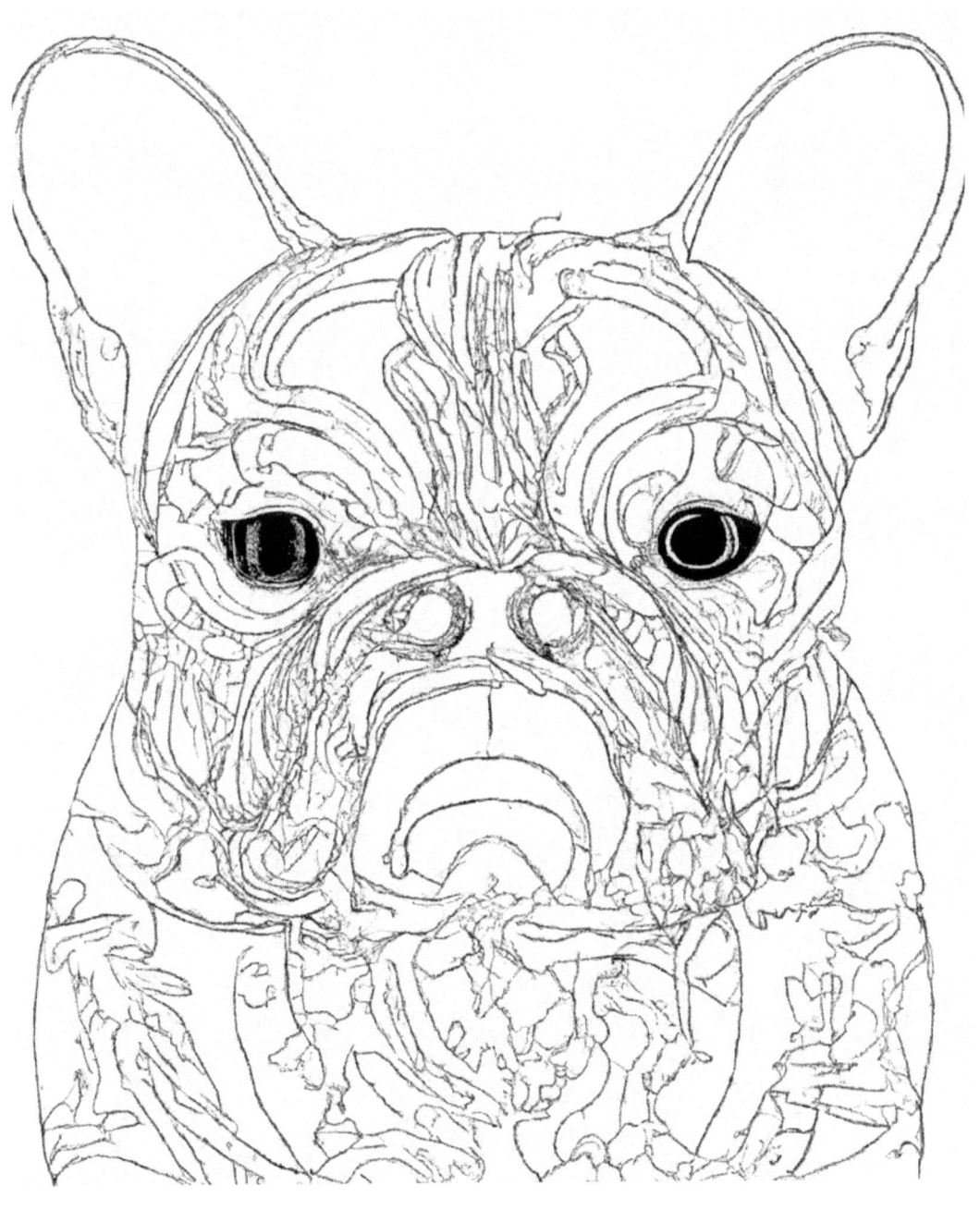

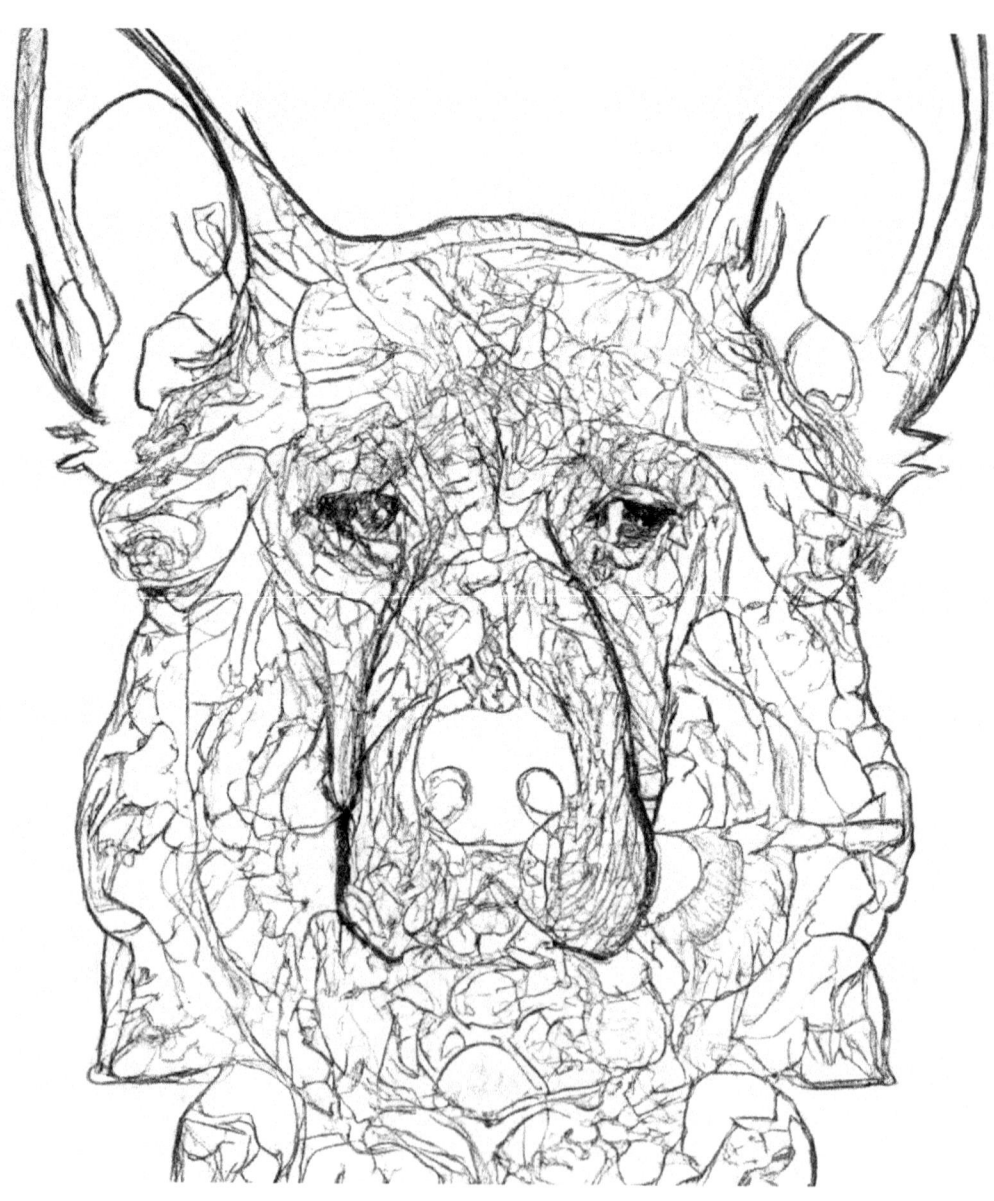

Some of the sample pictures from our other Books

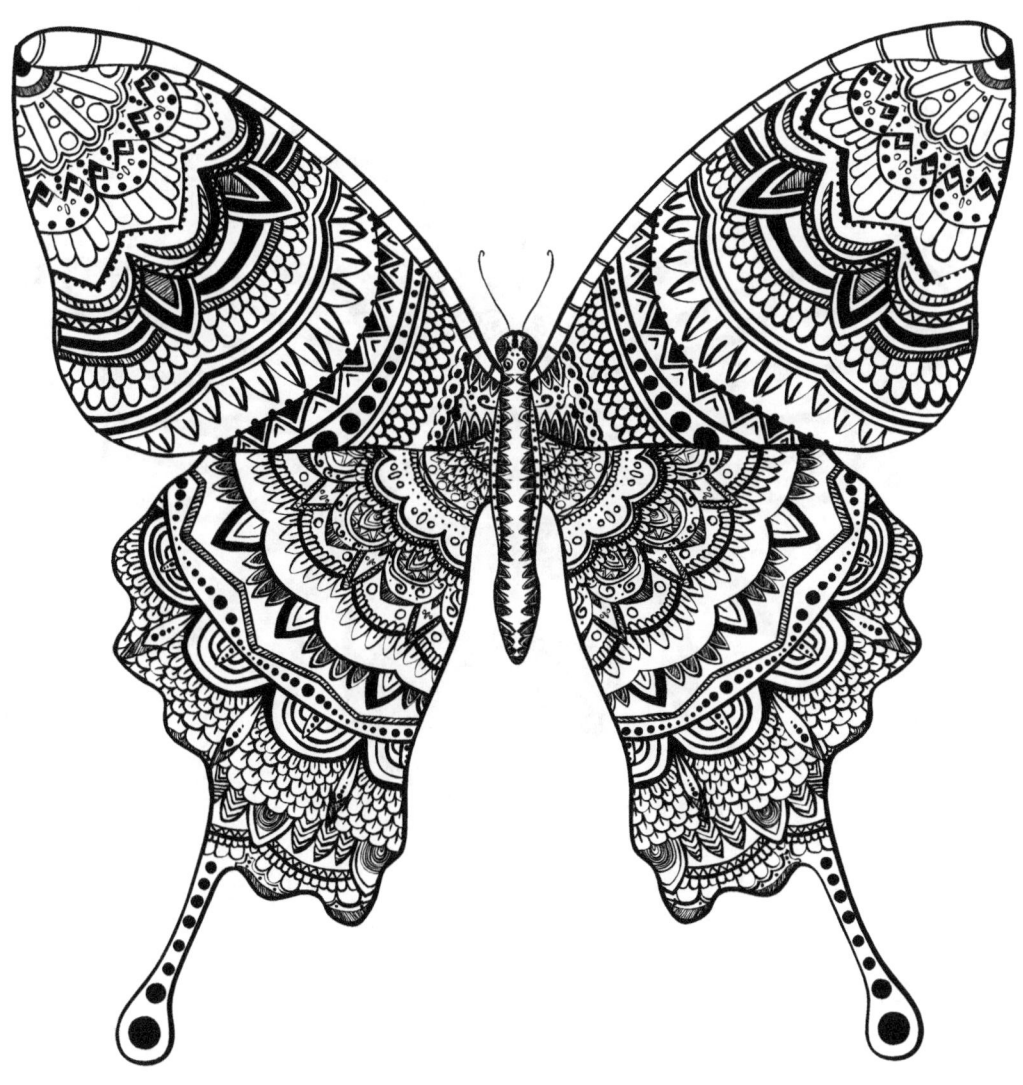

Some of the sample pictures
from our other Books

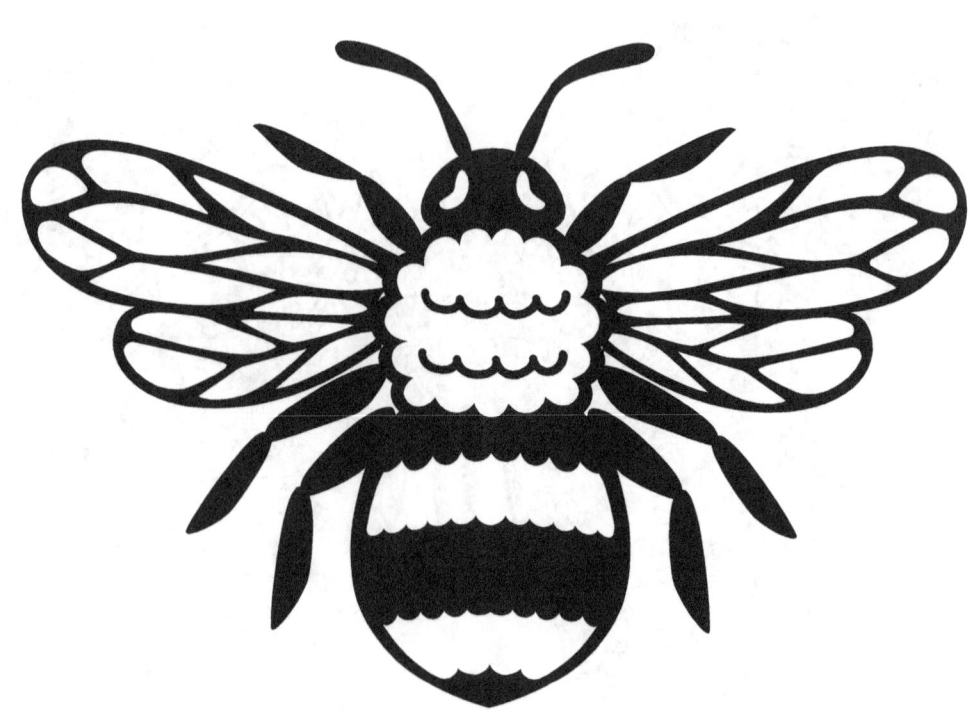

Some of the sample pictures from our other Books

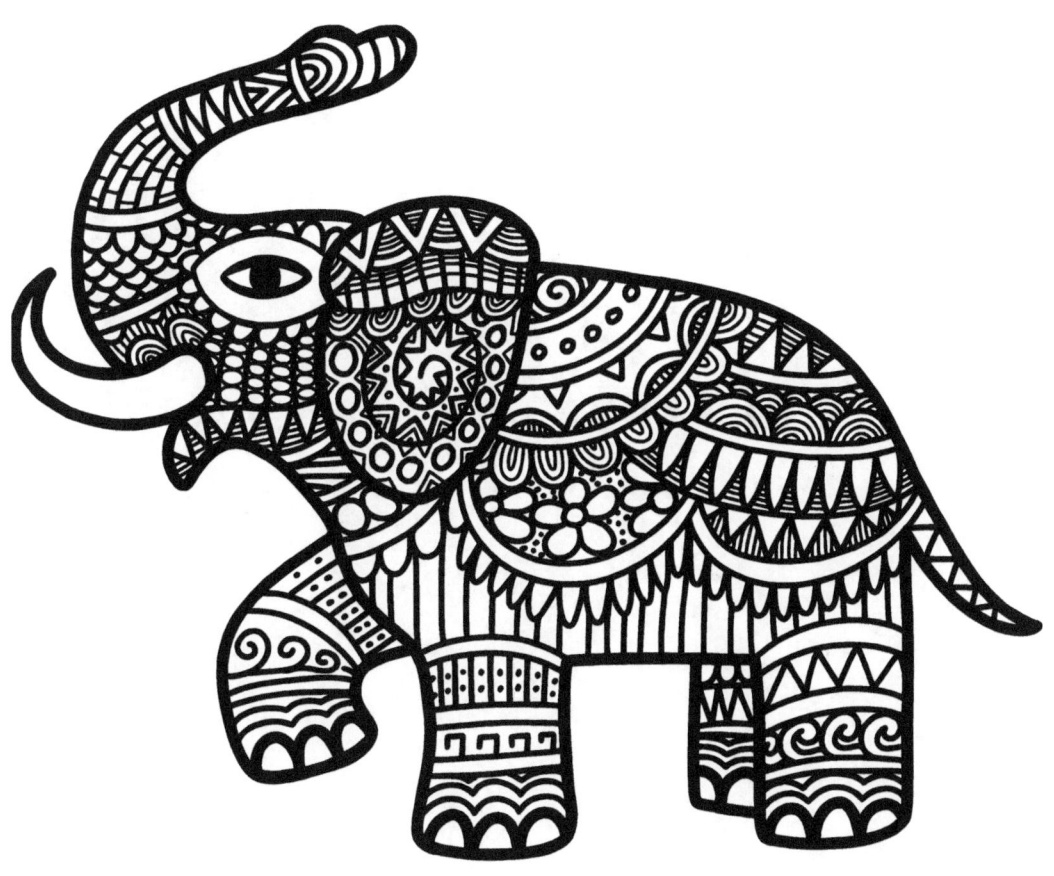

"THE **END** IS ONLY FOR THE BOOK NOT FOR THE ART"